What's Blocking Your Progress?

By

Brenda Diann Johnson

ASWIFTT ENTERPRISES, LLC
Duncanville, Texas 75138

Copyright © 2025 Brenda Diann Johnson

All rights reserved

No part of this book may be reproduced, stored in a retrieval system, or transmitted by any means, electronic, mechanical, photocopying, recording or otherwise, without written permission from the author.

Brenda Diann Johnson
E-mail: brendadiannjohnson@yahoo.com

Published by
ASWIFTT ENTERPRISES, LLC
Imprint: ASWIFTT BOOKS
P.O. Box 380669
Duncanville, Texas 75138-0669

ISBN: 979-8-9901107-8-6

Library of Congress Control Number: 2025938423

Printed in the United States of America

All scripture quotations are from the King James Version of the Bible unless otherwise noted.

Cover Design and Editing by Brenda Diann Johnson

Dedications

What's Blocking Your Progress? is dedicated to those who want to accomplish their dreams and goals and fulfill their God-Ordained Purpose.

Acknowledgments

I acknowledge an Almighty God who gave me the passion, creativity, ideas, and inventions to educate the masses. I am determined to be a good steward.

Table of Contents

Dedications..................................5
Acknowledgments..........................6
Introduction...............................11

Chapter I Inner Struggles.........15
Chapter II Outer Struggles........23
Chapter III Focus......................31
Chapter IV Disobedience.........37
Chapter V Discipline.................43

Chapter VI Consistency............51
Chapter VII Sin.........................57
Chapter VIII Alignment............63
Chapter IX Action....................71
Chapter X Roadmap and Tools...........79

About the Author......................85
Books and Services..................87

Introduction

10

Introduction

"It's Up to You To Get Your Dreams and Goals Moving"
Brenda Diann Johnson

Let's face it: everybody must overcome problems, challenges, and obstacles. No one is exempt from daily responsibilities or life issues. We must all learn how to accomplish tasks most efficiently.

Complaining and murmuring about our problems will not help us accomplish things; it only delays and hinders progress. No one is going to feel sorry for us if we don't take responsibility for solving our problems. My aunt Marie always told me growing up that no one in this world owes me anything. If they do help me, it's because they want to, not because they had to. This lesson instilled in me a deep sense of gratitude for the help I received. We must never forget that we are responsible for our own lives. On this journey, we will experience both mountaintop and valley moments. We must learn how to navigate through all of it with God's help so we can fulfill the purpose that God preordained for our lives.

Along this journey, we will encounter stumbling blocks, struggles, spiritual warfare, distractions, and setbacks that will challenge our progress in fulfilling our purpose. The objective is not to give up. Deciding not to give up is half the battle. The other half is figuring out what is blocking our progress so we can fix it. This process of identifying and overcoming obstacles is crucial in taking control of our journey. Then we can move forward successfully to accomplish our dreams, goals, and purpose.

Inner Struggles

Chapter I
Inner Struggles

Wherefore, my beloved, as ye have always obeyed, not as in my presence only, but now more in my absence, work out your own salvation with fear and trembling. (Philippians 2:12 KJV)

Overcoming inner struggles is not easy. Many of us are still dealing with the effects of childhood traumas, fears, doubts, insecurities, self-identity, self-worth, parental issues, rape, abuse, and the list goes on. Inner struggles are the emotional and psychological challenges we face within ourselves. When someone triggers our inner struggles, these issues resurface, and we must confront them again.

We often face internal battles that hinder us from reaching our full potential. The Bible offers guidance on overcoming inner challenges. Galatians 5:22-23 speak about the fruits of the Spirit, which include love, joy, peace, patience, kindness, goodness, faithfulness, gentleness, and self-control. Conversely, Galatians 5:19-21 warns against the deeds of the flesh, such as hatred, jealousy, and envy, which can manifest as external barriers (McCuddy et al., 2007). The fruits of the Spirit are virtues that promote a positive and harmonious way of living. They foster love, joy, and peace in our relationships and within ourselves. These traits encourage patience, kindness, and goodness that enable us to interact with others in a supportive and nurturing manner. Faithfulness, gentleness, and self-control provide a solid foundation for personal integrity and self-discipline.

In contrast, the deeds of the flesh represent negative behaviors that disrupt our peace and well-being. Hatred leads to conflict and division, jealousy breeds resentment, and envy fuels dissatisfaction and strife. These destructive emotions and actions can create barriers to personal growth and harmonious relationships. They hinder us from experiencing the fullness of life God intends for us.

Cultivating the fruits of the Spirit is essential for overcoming the deeds of the flesh. By focusing on love, joy, and peace, we can transform our internal struggles into opportunities for growth. Practicing patience, kindness, and goodness helps us to build strong and positive connections with others. Embracing faithfulness, gentleness, and self-control enables us to maintain our integrity with grace and navigate life's challenges.

Developing the fruits of the Spirit leads to a resilient mindset, enabling us to overcome internal obstacles and external barriers. It allows us to align ourselves with God's will, fostering a deep sense of purpose and fulfillment. By cultivating these virtues, we can reach our full potential and live a life that embodies God's love and grace.

Strongholds can also hinder our progress. A stronghold is where a particular belief or activity is vigorously defended or upheld. According to Jeffrey B. Krall, the anatomy of a stronghold includes addictions, anxieties, fears, overeating, drugs, pornography, promiscuity, gambling, jealousy, manipulation, alcoholism, gaming, and social media. These are idols we trust to give us a sense of peace and security. We rely on them because our souls are unsettled and anxious, fearing something more than we fear God. We don't truly know God's love because we believe a lie. (Krall, J., 2013)

To overcome strongholds, we must identify them and acknowledge their presence. Recognition is the first step towards healing. Once identified, we should surrender these strongholds to God, seeking His strength and guidance through prayer and scripture. Replacing these idols with God's truth and love will gradually break their hold on us. Building a supportive community that encourages spiritual growth and accountability can also aid in overcoming strongholds. (Kate L., 2024) Finally, continually reaffirming our trust in God and His promises will help us maintain freedom from these hindrances.

An impressive biblical example is David. Before becoming king, David faced immense inner struggles. Despite the anointing in his life, he experienced fear and doubt. He often ran from Saul to avoid being harmed. David displayed courage when he killed Goliath. His faith in God helped him overcome challenges, leading to his victory and ultimate kingship.

As we mature, we must also unlearn toxic teachings and behaviors that hold us captive. Romans 12:2 (NKJV) says, "And do not be conformed to this world, but be transformed by the renewing of your mind, that you may prove what is that good and acceptable and perfect will of God." To move forward, we must embrace new information and align with God.

References

McCuddy, M., & Pirie, W. (2007). Spirituality, stewardship, and financial decision-making. Managerial Finance, 33(12), 957-969.

Kate L. August 18, 2024. Holistic Approaches To Rehab - How New Dawn Treatment Centers Integrate Mind, Body, And Spirit In Recovery - New Dawn Treatment Centers | Northern California Rehab. https://www.newdawntreatmentcenters.com/holistic-rehab-mind-body-spirit-integration-at-new-dawn/

Krall, Jeffrey B. https://onelordonebody.com/2013/11/19/the-anatomy-of-a-stronghold/

20

Outer Struggles

22

Chapter II
Outer Struggles

"You are the most important person that you will talk to all day." Zig Zigler

In the journey toward personal growth and success, individuals often encounter numerous external obstacles that can impede their progress. These outer struggles include societal pressures, financial constraints, unsupportive relationships, physical limitations, and environmental factors. Understanding and navigating these challenges is essential for moving forward and achieving one's goals. This chapter explores the nature of these external obstacles, provides examples, and highlights the importance of seeking guidance and maintaining faith to overcome them.

Societal pressure, a force that can shape an individual's decisions and actions, is a significant external obstacle. It can take many forms, from the pressure to conform to cultural norms to the desire to fit in with peer groups. For instance, the expectation of pursuing higher education and securing a well-paying job can lead to stress and anxiety for those with alternative career aspirations.

The fear of judgment and rejection can hinder individuals from pursuing their passions and living authentically.

Overcoming societal pressures requires self-awareness, confidence, and the courage to make choices that align with one's values and goals. Empowerment from making these choices can be a source of inspiration and motivation. (Faye, D.)

Financial constraints, another significant external obstacle, can block progress. Limited financial resources can prevent individuals from accessing education, healthcare, and opportunities for personal and professional growth. (VTI) For instance, the inability to afford tuition fees may restrict someone from pursuing higher education, thereby limiting their career prospects. Additionally, financial instability can lead to stress and affect mental health, making it difficult to focus on long-term goals. Overcoming financial constraints often requires strategic planning, budgeting, and exploring alternative funding sources, such as scholarships, grants, or loans. It also requires resilience and the ability to adapt to changing circumstances. (Command Wear.com) Emphasizing the importance of resilience in this context can make us feel determined and hopeful.

Unsupportive relationships can also hinder progress by creating a hostile and discouraging environment. These relationships may involve friends, family members, or colleagues who do not believe in one's abilities or aspirations.

For example, a person may have a partner criticizing their career choices or a family member undermining their confidence. Such relationships can lead to self-doubt, decreased motivation, and a lack of support during times of challenge. It is crucial to recognize the impact of unsupportive relationships and take steps to distance oneself from individuals who bring harm or negativity. Building a supportive network of people who encourage and uplift is essential for achieving progress. (Longlifenutri.com) Stressing the role of faith in overcoming these relationships can make us feel comforted and reassured.

Physical limitations refer to the challenges posed by health issues or disabilities that can affect an individual's ability to perform specific tasks or achieve certain goals. These limitations can range from chronic illnesses to mobility impairments. For instance, an individual with a physical disability may face difficulties accessing specific public spaces or participating in physical activities.

Overcoming physical limitations requires determination, adaptability, and seeking appropriate medical care and support. It also involves advocating for accessibility and inclusion to ensure equal opportunities for individuals with disabilities.

Environmental factors encompass external conditions and surroundings that can influence progress. These factors can include natural disasters, political instability, and socioeconomic conditions. For example, living in an area prone to frequent natural disasters can disrupt daily life and hinder long-term planning. Political instability may limit access to resources and opportunities, while socioeconomic conditions can affect education and employment prospects. Overcoming environmental factors requires resilience, proactive planning, and seeking support from community and government resources. It also involves being adaptable and finding innovative solutions to navigate challenging circumstances.

In addition to understanding these external obstacles, individuals must learn to solve their problems to move forward. Unfortunate circumstances are inevitable, but developing problem-solving skills and seeking guidance can make a significant difference in how you cope. (Dr. Lena Pearlman)

According to 1 Corinthians 15:33, "Do not be misled: Bad company corrupts good character." This biblical principle emphasizes the importance of surrounding oneself with positive influences and removing oneself from harmful relationships. Seeking God's guidance and maintaining faith can provide the strength and direction needed to overcome external struggles.

A prominent example of triumph over external obstacles through divine guidance is the biblical story of Joseph. Joseph faced numerous external struggles, from being sold into slavery by his brothers to false accusations and imprisonment. Despite these challenges, his unwavering faith and integrity enabled him to rise to a position of power in Egypt. Joseph's story illustrates the importance of maintaining faith, seeking divine guidance, and persevering through difficult circumstances. His journey is a testament to the power of resilience and the potential to overcome external struggles and achieve progress.

In conclusion, external struggles, including societal pressures, financial constraints, unsupportive relationships, physical limitations, and environmental factors, can hinder progress and personal growth. Understanding and developing strategies to navigate these challenges is essential for moving forward. Seeking guidance, maintaining faith, and surrounding oneself with positive influences can provide the strength and resilience needed to overcome external obstacles. By addressing these challenges and finding effective solutions, individuals can achieve their goals and realize their full potential. (Emotionalscan.com)

References

Faye, D. M. Dating with Social Anxiety: Overcoming Challenges. https://careclinic.io/dating-with-social-anxiety/

VTI, Ensuring Vocational Training Is Accessible to All - Vocational Training Institute. https://instituteofvocationaltraining.com/ensuring-vocational-training-is-accessible-to-all/

Command Wear.com, Persistency vs Consistency: Key Differences Explained. https://commandwear.com/persistency-vs-consistency-key-differences-explained/

Longlifenutri.com, https://www.longlifenutri.com/blogs/news/breaking-free-from-the-obesity-mental-health-loop

Dr. Lena Pearlman & Associates, Mental Health & Summer: Understanding Seasonal ImpactsPearlman & Associates. https://stlmentalhealth.com/mental-health-and-the-impact-of-summer/

Emotionalscan.com. April 3, 2023. Motivation - Have you ever seen your emotions? - Emotional Scan. https://emotionalscan.com/2023/04/03/motivation/

Focus

Chapter III
Focus

"Wherefore seeing we also are compassed about with so great a cloud of witnesses, let us lay aside every weight, and the sin which doth so easily beset us, and let us run with patience the race that is set before us." (Hebrews 12:1 KJV)

Focus is the ability to concentrate on a specific task or objective without being distracted by external or internal factors. (w8md.com) It involves directing one's attention and efforts towards a singular goal, ensuring that all actions are aligned with achieving that goal. Maintaining focus is essential for making progress, achieving dreams, and fulfilling one's purpose.

One of the primary benefits of staying focused is increased productivity. When individuals concentrate on their tasks, they complete them more efficiently and with higher quality. Focus enhances problem-solving skills, allowing the mind to delve deeply into a subject and uncover solutions that may not be apparent when distracted. Additionally, staying focused reduces stress, as it simultaneously prevents the mind from becoming overwhelmed by juggling multiple tasks. Consequently, individuals who maintain focus are more likely to experience a profound sense of accomplishment and deep satisfaction, knowing they have given their best to their tasks.

Conversely, the inability to stay focused can have detrimental consequences. Distractions can lead to procrastination, causing tasks to pile up and deadlines to be missed. A lack of focus can lead to poor-quality work, as attention is divided and errors become more frequent. (Hewson, C, 2019) Furthermore, when distractions hinder progress, it can lead to frustration and a waning motivation to pursue goals. Proverbs 4:25-27 advises, "Let your eyes look straight ahead; fix your gaze directly before you. Give careful thought to the paths for your feet and be steadfast in all your ways. Do not turn to the right or the left; keep your foot from evil." This scripture emphasizes the importance of unwavering focus in establishing one's ways and achieving success, instilling a sense of determination and commitment in the reader.

Staying focused is crucial in achieving your goals and dreams. It fosters a profound sense of clarity and direction, enabling individuals to make informed decisions that align with their objectives. Focus allows one to prioritize tasks effectively, ensuring time and resources are allocated toward activities that contribute to goal attainment. Individuals can overcome obstacles and setbacks by maintaining focus, as their determination propels them forward. Ultimately, staying focused on God's plan provides the guidance necessary to achieve dreams, goals, and purpose, as His direction is infallible.

Distractions and a lack of clarity can derail progress, causing individuals to stumble and lose sight of their goals. When people allow distractions to interfere with their focus, it can lead to confusion and a scattered approach to tasks. This can result in wasted time and effort, and the individual may be off course. Proverbs 4:25-27 offers wisdom to prevent distractions from causing one to stumble and ensure that their path remains established.

The biblical figure Nehemiah exemplifies remarkable focus while rebuilding the walls of Jerusalem. Despite facing opposition and numerous distractions, Nehemiah remained steadfast in his mission. Guided by prayer and reliance on God, he persevered in his efforts, ultimately achieving his goal. The story of Nehemiah's determination and focus can be found in the Book of Nehemiah in the Bible, specifically in chapters 1 through 6. His unwavering focus is a powerful testament to staying dedicated to one's purpose, regardless of the challenges that may be encountered.

References

Hewson, Claire. September 10, 2029. Why is sleep important for academic success? https://tutormykids.co.uk/2019/09/10/why-is-sleep-important-for-academic-success/

W8MD.com weight loss and sleep centers. https://w8md.com/wiki/Focus

Disobedience

Chapter IV
Disobedience

And Samuel said, Hath the LORD as great delight in burnt offerings and sacrifices, as in obeying the voice of the LORD? Behold, to obey is better than sacrifice, and to hearken than the fat of rams. (1 Samuel 15:22 KJV)

Disobedience, the refusal or failure to follow rules, commands, or instructions, often leads to stagnation and setbacks in various aspects of life. In a spiritual context, disobeying God's commandments hinders progress and blessings. The Bible emphasizes the importance of obedience to God's will, highlighting both the rewards for compliance and the consequences of defiance. (Garcia, K., 2024)

Disobedience to God can manifest in various ways, including ignoring His commandments, neglecting prayer, failing to live according to His teachings, and engaging in actions contrary to His moral principles. These acts of defiance create spiritual barriers and impede personal and communal growth. As stated in 1 Samuel 15:22, 'But Samuel replied: 'Does the Lord delight in burnt offerings and sacrifices as much as in obeying the Lord? To obey is better than sacrifice, and to heed is better than the fat of rams.' This scripture underscores the primacy of obedience over ritualistic acts.

The consequences of disobedience are clearly outlined in the Bible. James 4:17 states, 'If anyone knows the good they ought to do and doesn't do it, it is sin for them.' Furthermore, Deuteronomy 28:15 warns, 'However, if you do not obey the Lord your God and do not carefully follow all his commands and decrees, I am giving you today, all these curses will come on you and overtake you.' These passages highlight the severity of disobedience, which can lead to various forms of suffering and loss. It's a stark reminder of the importance of obedience and the caution we should exercise in our actions. (King, P., 2023)

The story of Jonah is a poignant example of the consequences and rewards of obedience. Jonah initially disobeyed God's command to go to Nineveh and fled to Tarshish. This act of defiance led to several calamities, including a violent storm and Jonah being swallowed by a great fish. Jonah 1:3 states, "But Jonah ran away from the Lord and headed for Tarshish. He went down to Joppa, where he found a ship bound for that port." However, upon repenting and obeying God's command, Jonah was released and successfully fulfilled his mission in Nineveh. Jonah 3:3-4 declares, "Jonah obeyed the word of the Lord and went to Nineveh.

Disobedience to God's commandments undoubtedly creates barriers to success and progress. By understanding the significance of obedience, as illustrated in the scriptures, individuals can align their actions with God's will and remove obstacles hindering their growth. The story of Jonah serves as a testament to the transformative power of obedience in overcoming challenges and achieving divine purpose. Ultimately, aligning oneself with God's commandments paves the way to blessings and fulfillment, while defiance leads to adversity and stagnation. This understanding empowers us to overcome challenges and achieve our divine purpose.

References

Garcia, Kenneth. How The Just Shall Live By Faith According To Bible (2024). https://www.biblekeeper.com/the-just-shall-live-by-faith/

King, Paul. September 18, 2023. Did Nadab And Abihu Go To Heaven. https://nwaonline.org/did-nadab-and-abihu-go-to-heaven/

Discipline

Chapter V
Discipline

But I discipline my body and bring it into subjection, lest, when I have preached to others, I myself should become disqualified. (1 Corinthians 9:27)

Discipline is a tool and a source of empowerment that allows us to achieve our goals and aspirations. It provides a structured and organized approach to life's challenges, instilling a profound sense of control and confidence. (Sostar, M. et al., 2023) Proverbs 12:1 states, "Whoever loves discipline loves knowledge, but whoever hates correction is stupid." This scripture underscores the value of loving discipline and acquiring knowledge. By embracing a disciplined lifestyle rooted in biblical principles, we not only persevere in adversity but also thrive in it.

To further illustrate the significance of discipline, we can examine the life of Daniel. Daniel's disciplined prayer life and unwavering commitment to God's laws were instrumental in his prosperity in Babylon despite numerous plots against him. Daniel 6:10 depicts his consistent prayer routine: "When Daniel learned that the decree had been published, he went home to his upstairs room where the windows opened toward Jerusalem. Three times a day, he knelt and prayed, giving thanks to his God, just as he had done before." This scripture highlights the importance of maintaining a disciplined spiritual practice, regardless of external circumstances. (Stefanovic, Z. et al., 2004)

Another scripture that emphasizes the importance of discipline is Hebrews 12:11, which states, "No discipline seems pleasant at the time, but painful. Later on, however, it produces a harvest of righteousness and peace for those trained by it." This verse speaks to the enduring benefits of discipline, acknowledging the temporary discomfort it may bring but ultimately yielding positive outcomes. It encourages believers to endure the challenges of disciplined living, instilling a sense of hope and optimism that it will lead to righteousness and peace.

However, it's important to note that discipline is not about being rigid or inflexible. It's about having a clear direction and consistently staying on course. It's about learning from mistakes and being open to correction. This verse serves as a reminder that ignoring discipline and instruction can result in negative consequences, whereas embracing correction leads to honor and success.

When the benefits of discipline are compared to the consequences of indiscipline, the urgency of embracing discipline becomes clear. Discipline fosters a sense of responsibility, consistency, and resilience, which is essential for overcoming obstacles and reaching one's full potential. On the other hand, an undisciplined approach can lead to missed opportunities, setbacks, and failure. The contrast is stark, and it serves as a call to action for us to choose discipline.

For instance, discipline in managing time, such as setting a daily schedule and sticking to it, can lead to a more productive life. Similarly, discipline in managing finances, like budgeting and saving, can lead to financial stability. In relationships, discipline can be demonstrated through consistent communication and mutual respect, ultimately leading to stronger bonds. (Burt, C., 2020)

Regarding health, maintaining a balanced diet and engaging in regular exercise can lead to a healthier and more fulfilling life. (Hopley, K.) Maintaining discipline is difficult, especially in adversity or when the results do not seem immediate. It requires patience, perseverance, and a strong belief in the long-term benefits. However, remember that discipline is a journey, not a destination. It's about the daily choices and actions that lead to long-term success. In conclusion, discipline is not just a means to an end but a way of life. Developing a disciplined lifestyle rooted in biblical principles is essential for achieving goals and making progress. Proverbs 12:1 and Hebrews 12:11 emphasize the importance of embracing loving discipline and persevering through challenges for the sake of righteousness and peace. Daniel's disciplined prayer life is a powerful example of how an unwavering commitment to God can lead to prosperity, even in the face of adversity. (Daskal, L.) By embracing discipline, individuals can unlock their true potential and navigate life's challenges with confidence and success.

References

Šostar, M., Šostar, M., & Ristanović, V. (2023). An Assessment of the Impact of the COVID-19 Pandemic on Consumer Behavior Using the Analytic Hierarchy Process Model. Sustainability, 15(20), 15104.

Stefanovic, Z., & Pröbstle, M. (2004). Zdravko Stefanovic. https://core.ac.uk/download/511301132.pdf

John 15. Rocks, February 19, 2023. Four kinds of prayer posture and position in the Bible - John15.Rocks. https://www.john15.rocks/four-kinds-of-prayer-posture-and-position-in-the-bible/

Burt, Coleena. April 18, 2020 AUdapting: Simons Shares Insights on Remote Teaching – College of Architecture, Design and Construction. https://cadc.auburn.edu/audapting-simons-shares-insights-on-remote-teaching/

Hopley, Kelly. The Power Duo: Achieving Optimal Well-being Through Diet and Exercise - Incorporating Wellness with Kelly Hopley. https://incorporatingwellnesswithkellyhopley.com/the-power-duo-achieving-optimal-well-being-through-diet-and-exercise/

Daskal, Lolly. Why Leaders Must Stay Positive Even When the Future Looks Bleak - Lolly Daskal. https://www.lollydaskal.com/leadership/why-leaders-must-stay-positive-even-when-the-future-looks-bleak/

Consistency

Chapter VI
Consistency

And let us not be weary in well doing: for in due season we shall reap, if we faint not. (Galatians 6:9 KJV)

Consistency can be defined as the steadfast adherence to the same principles, course, or form over time. (Florkin, J., 2024) It involves maintaining commitment and effort regardless of external circumstances or challenges. This quality is integral to pursuing any goal or objective, ensuring that progress is sustained and achievements are meaningful and lasting.

The rewards of consistency are numerous. By being consistent, individuals can build trust and credibility, both personally and professionally. This reliability fosters stronger relationships and enhances reputation, allowing people to rely on one another. Consistency also yields incremental progress as persistent efforts accumulate over time, ultimately leading to significant accomplishments. Conversely, inconsistency can have detrimental consequences. It can lead to a lack of trust, reliability, and erratic progress that hinders long-term achievements. Inconsistency breeds uncertainty and can result in missed opportunities and wasted resources.

Consistency plays a crucial role in facilitating progress. When efforts are consistently applied, skills are refined, knowledge is expanded, and goals are approached methodically. This steady advancement enables individuals to overcome obstacles, adapt to changing circumstances, and achieve their objectives. (Martin, T., 2021) Maintaining a consistent approach ensures that each step is purposeful and aligned with their mission.

The significance of consistency is highlighted in Galatians 6:9, which encourages believers not to grow weary in doing good, for in due season, they will reap a harvest if they do not give up. This scripture underscores the importance of perseverance and steadfastness in our efforts. Being consistent aligns us with the right time, allowing us to experience the rewards of our dedication and hard work. (Benson, L., 2024)

Paul's missionary work and teachings provide a profound example of the importance of consistency in achieving one's mission. Despite facing numerous hardships, including imprisonment, beatings, and shipwrecks, Paul remained unwavering in his commitment to spreading the gospel. His persistent efforts transformed the early church and laid the foundation for Christianity's growth. Scriptures such as Acts 20:19-24 and 2 Timothy 4:7-8 illustrate Paul's consistency and dedication to his mission. In Acts 20:19-24, Paul speaks of serving the Lord with

humility and tears despite his trials.
In 2 Timothy 4:7-8, he reflects on having fought the good fight and finished the race, demonstrating his unwavering commitment to his calling.

In conclusion, consistency is a fundamental quality that underpins long-term success. It involves maintaining a steadfast commitment to one's principles and efforts, resulting in trust, credibility, and incremental progress. Galatians 6:9 encourages us to persevere in doing good, promising a harvest in due season. Paul's consistent missionary work and teachings exemplify the transformative power of persistence, highlighting the importance of consistency in achieving one's mission and aligning with God's timing. (Amo, H., 2024)

References

Florkin, J. (2024) https://julienflorkin.com/self-improvement/personal-development/consistency-2/

Benson, Lily. March 19, 2024. Pressing On Archives | Christian Learning & News. https://www.christianlearning.com/tag/pressing-on/

Amo, H. November 16, 2024. CONTINUE TO DO GOOD – Dr. Henry Amo MD. https://drhenryamo.com/continue-to-do-good/

Martin, T. (2021). The effects of collaborative leadership practices on employee satisfaction levels. https://core.ac.uk/download/459195617.pdf

Sin

Chapter VII
Sin

For the wages of sin is death; but the gift of God is eternal life through Jesus Christ our Lord. (Romans 6:23 KJV)

Sin, as described in the Bible, is a significant barrier to human progress. It separates us from God and leads to various negative consequences. Hebrews 12:1 admonishes us to "lay aside every weight, and the sin which doth so easily beset us." This phrase 'lay aside every weight' can be understood as removing any burden or obstacle that hinders our spiritual and personal growth, highlighting the importance of shedding sin. (Criswell, W., 1960) This chapter examines the benefits of abstaining from sin and its consequences, as well as the biblical figures who either abstained from or freely sinned.

Abstaining from sin yields numerous benefits, foremost among them maintaining a strong relationship with God. Proverbs 6:16-19 lists the seven sins that God hates: "A proud look, a lying tongue, hands that shed innocent blood, a heart that devises wicked plans, feet that are swift in running to evil." The phrase 'swift in running to evil' can be understood as a quick and eager participation in sinful activities. Avoiding these sins helps believers stay aligned with God's will and ensures their paths remain unobstructed. Moreover, seeking forgiveness and striving for righteousness, as indicated in Romans 3:23, can restore our relationship with God and eliminate hindrances. This is further emphasized in 1 John 1:9, which states, 'If we confess our sins, he is faithful and just and will forgive us our sins and purify us from all unrighteousness.' (Towns, E., 2007)

In contrast, indulging in sin leads to spiritual and material consequences. The story of David and Bathsheba, as recounted in 2 Samuel 11-12, serves as a profound example. David's sin of adultery with Bathsheba and the subsequent murder of her husband, Uriah, led to severe repercussions. (Crosstalk.com) The immediate consequence was the death of their child, as found in 2 Samuel 12:14. Despite his grievous sins, David's heartfelt repentance and plea for forgiveness, as shown in Psalm 51, allowed him to find redemption and restore his path with God. This powerful demonstration of the transformative power of sincere repentance offers hope and inspiration to all who seek forgiveness, showing that no sin is too great for God's grace.

A comparison of biblical figures who abstained from sin with those who freely indulged in it further elucidates the impact of sin on progress. Joseph, found in Genesis, is a prime example of righteousness. Despite facing numerous trials, including being sold into slavery by his brothers

(Genesis 37:28) and being falsely accused by Potiphar's wife (Genesis 39:7-20), Joseph remained faithful to God. His steadfastness led to his rise as Egypt's second most powerful man, showcasing how abstaining from sin and remaining righteous can lead to success and progress. This emphasis on the role of righteousness in success can motivate and encourage the audience in their spiritual journey, showing that God rewards those who remain faithful. Conversely, figures such as King Saul, who repeatedly disobeyed God's commands (1 Samuel 13:13-14), faced the loss of his kingdom and eventual downfall, illustrating the detrimental effects of sin.

In conclusion, sin undeniably blocks progress by severing our connection with God and leading to adverse outcomes. However, the Bible also teaches that seeking forgiveness and striving for righteousness can restore our relationship with God and remove obstacles. The contrasting lives of biblical figures who either abstained from or indulged in sin highlight the significance of adhering to God's commandments for a prosperous and fulfilling life. This stress on the importance of God's commandments can make the audience feel guided and reassured in their spiritual journey, knowing that God's word is a reliable and unwavering guide. As Hebrews 12:1 and Romans 3:23 remind us, laying aside sin and seeking redemption are crucial steps toward spiritual growth and progress.

References

Crosstalk.com, Did God approve of David and Solomon having multiple wives? https://biblechat.ai/knowledgebase/christian-living/ethics-morality/did-god-approve-david-solomon-having-multiple-wives/

Criswell, W. A. (1960). Stripping for the Race, February 21, 1960. – W. A. Criswell Sermon Library. https://wacriswell.com/sermon-topic/race/

Towns, E. L. (2007). What Makes You Do the Things You Do?: Lesson 4. https://core.ac.uk/download/58823582.docx

Alignment

Chapter VIII
Alignment

But seek ye first the kingdom of God, and his righteousness, and all these things shall be added unto you.
(Matthew 6:33 KJV)

God's divine principles, also known as His laws and teachings, are designed to guide us toward a life of profound fulfillment, deep peace, and lasting prosperity. Aligning our lives with these principles ensures that we are on the correct path, while nonalignment can lead to chaos, confusion, and suffering. The scriptures offer wisdom and guidance on living by God's will. One such scripture is Matthew 6:33, which says, "But seek ye first the kingdom of God, and his righteousness; and all these things shall be added unto you." (KJV)

When we align our lives with God's principles, we experience immense benefits. Proverbs 3:5-6 instruct us to trust in the Lord and acknowledge Him in all our ways so that He will direct our paths: "Trust in the Lord with all thine heart; and lean not unto thine own understanding. In all thy ways acknowledge him, and he shall direct thy paths." (KJV) This alignment ensures that our decisions, actions, and thoughts are in harmony with the divine will, leading to a life of clear purpose and unwavering direction.

One of the most profound examples of living in alignment with God's principles is found in the life of King Solomon. Solomon's wisdom and strict adherence to God's principles brought Israel unprecedented prosperity and peace. His reign is a living testament to the blessings of living in accordance with God's will. In 1 Kings 3:9-14, Solomon asks God for wisdom to govern the people, and God grants him wisdom, wealth, and honor. This passage is a beacon of hope, illustrating the rewards of seeking God's guidance.

On the other hand, when we fail to align our lives with God's principles, a state of nonalignment results. This can lead to adverse consequences. When we ignore divine guidance, we expose ourselves to turmoil, strife, and misdirection. The Bible is replete with examples of individuals and nations that faced dire consequences as a result of their departure from God's will. (ICN) Proverbs 14:12 warns us, "There is a way which seemeth right unto a man, but the end thereof are the ways of death." (KJV) This scripture highlights the dangers of relying on our understanding rather than seeking divine guidance. (Walker, L., 2022)

The story of Solomon also serves as a cautionary tale. Despite his initial adherence to God's principles, Solomon eventually strayed from God's path by marrying foreign women and worshipping their gods. This led to the division of the kingdom and numerous conflicts. 1 Kings 11:1-13 details Solomon's downfall, emphasizing the consequences of nonalignment with God's will.

Aligning our lives with God's principles involves consciously seeking His kingdom and righteousness. This is not just a suggestion but a divine promise. Matthew 6:33 reminds us that when we prioritize God in our lives, He will provide for our needs: "But seek ye first the kingdom of God, and his righteousness; and all these things shall be added unto you." (KJV) This scripture encapsulates the essence of aligning with God's principles — putting Him first ensures everything else falls into place, making us feel secure and cared for.

Furthermore, Proverbs 3:5-6 serves as a practical guide for aligning with God's will. By trusting in the Lord and acknowledging Him in every aspect of our lives, we allow God to lead us on the right path. This alignment requires humility, faith, and a willingness to relinquish control to God. (Reynoso, R.)

The benefits of aligning with God's principles are manifold, including peace, prosperity, and divine guidance. Conversely, the consequences of nonalignment can be dire, leading to confusion, conflict, and hardship. The scriptures provide clear instructions on how to live by God's will, with examples such as Solomon's reign illustrating both the rewards of obedience and the consequences of disobedience. By seeking God's kingdom and righteousness first and trusting in His direction, we can ensure that our lives are aligned with His divine principles. (Glimmerglass, 1986)

References

ICN, Purpose – International Christian News | Christ Today. https://internationalchristiannews.org/tag/purpose/

Walker, Lynn. January 27, 2022. The Pastors Porch – Chickasha Today. https://www.chickashatoday.com/2022/01/27/the-pastors-porch-12/

Reynoso, Rondall. 18 Powerful Surrender Bible Verses - Faith on View. https://www.faithonview.com/surrender-bible-verses/

Glimmerglass Volume 45 Number 10 (1986). https://core.ac.uk/download/225552238.pdf

Action

Chapter IX
Action

For as the body without the Spirit is dead, so faith without works is dead also. (James 2:26 KJV)

Taking action on our dreams, goals, and purpose is not just a choice but a powerful tool for success and fulfillment in life. When we actively pursue our aspirations, we open the door to many benefits that can transform our lives. This empowerment is evident in the Bible's emphasis on action through scriptures such as "Faith without works is dead" (James 2:17) and "Man plans his way, but it is God's purpose that will prevail" (Proverbs 19:21). By integrating the formula of Pray, Plan, Prepare, and Execute, we can effectively harness the power of action to achieve our goals, feeling confident and in control.

The benefits of taking action on our dreams, goals, and purpose are manifold. First and foremost, action brings clarity. When working towards our aspirations, we gain a deeper understanding of what we truly want and how to achieve it. Additionally, taking action builds momentum. Each step we take propels us forward, making it easier to move in the right direction. Moreover, action fosters growth. We develop new skills and strengthen our resilience as we encounter challenges and overcome obstacles. And finally, taking action leads to the ultimate reward-achievement. When we persistently work towards our goals, we are more likely to succeed and experience the joy of accomplishment, which inspires and motivates us to continue our journey.

Failing to take action, on the other hand, hinders progress and can have detrimental consequences. When we procrastinate or remain inactive, our dreams and goals remain unfulfilled. This lack of progress can lead to frustration, self-doubt, and disconnection from our purpose. Furthermore, failing to take action can result in missed opportunities. When we fail to seize the moment, we may miss opportunities that could have propelled us forward.

Additionally, inaction can stifle our potential. Without the challenges and growth that come with taking action, we fail to develop the skills and resilience needed to achieve our dreams. Ultimately, failing to take action can lead to a life of regret as we realize the opportunities we have let slip away. This realization should fuel our determination and focus, pushing us to take action and avoid such sadness.

The Bible highlights the importance of action in achieving our goals and fulfilling our purpose. James 2:17 states that "faith without works is dead," emphasizing that belief alone is not enough; we must also take action to bring our dreams to life.

Implementing our plans and stepping forward in faith activates God's promises. Proverbs 19:21 reminds us that "Man plans his way, but it is God's purpose that will prevail," underscoring the need for action while recognizing that our efforts are guided by divine purpose. (thatsgrace.org) The story of Moses leading the Israelites out of Egypt is a powerful example of taking action despite initial reluctance. Moses' courage and obedience to God brought deliverance and fulfillment of God's promises (Exodus 3:10-12). Another example of Moses taking action is when he struck the rock to provide water for the Israelites, demonstrating God's provision through obedience (Numbers 20:7-11).

To effectively take action on our dreams, goals, and purpose, we can follow the formula of Pray, Plan, Prepare, and Execute. Pray involves seeking divine guidance and wisdom, aligning our aspirations with God's will. This divine support is a crucial part of the plan. The plan entails setting clear objectives and devising a strategy to achieve them. Preparing requires gathering resources, honing skills, and anticipating challenges. Finally, Execution is putting our plans into motion and taking decisive steps towards our goals. This formula ensures that our actions are purposeful and guided by faith, reassuring us that we are not alone in our journey.

In conclusion, action is necessary to achieve our goals, dreams, and purpose. The benefits of action include clarity, momentum, growth, and achievement, while the consequences of inaction are stagnation, missed opportunities, stifled potential, and regret. The Bible underscores the importance of action with scriptures such as James 2:17 and Proverbs 19:21, as well as examples like Moses leading the Israelites out of Egypt. By following the Pray, Plan, Prepare, and Execute formula, we can effectively take action and fulfill our God-given purpose. Let us be inspired to move forward with faith and determination, knowing that our actions can help us realize our dreams and fulfill our purpose.

References

Thatsgrace.org, Overcoming The Fear Of Obedience - Grace Church. https://thatsgrace.org/messages/overcoming-the-fear-of-obedience-west-bridgewater/

Roadmap and Tools

78

Chapter X
Roadmap and Tools

For which of you, intending to build a tower, sitteth not down first, and counteth the cost, whether he have sufficient to finish it? (Luke 14:28)

Achieving dreams, goals, and purpose requires a systematic approach, and the roadmap to success encompasses several mandatory tools. The first crucial step is separation. Separation involves distancing oneself from distractions and negative influences that can hinder progress. This tool helps create an environment conducive to growth and focus, essential for maintaining clarity and direction toward one's objectives.

The next set of tools is spiritual: God and the Holy Spirit. Believing in a higher power can provide guidance, inspiration, and strength. The Bible's blueprint provides principles, values, and morals as the foundation for informed decision-making and responsible actions. Adhering to these principles ensures one's journey is rooted in integrity and provides a sense of purpose that inspires and drives the path forward.

Knowledge and a plan are indispensable tools for any project. Knowledge involves acquiring information and skills necessary to understand and execute tasks effectively. A plan outlines the steps to achieve the desired outcome, breaking the project into manageable tasks. The correct mindset, focus, and strategies are also crucial. A positive attitude keeps one motivated, focus ensures attention to detail, and strategies provide methods to overcome obstacles and optimize performance.

Systems, hardware, and software are the technical tools for efficient project management. Systems refer to organized procedures that streamline processes. Hardware and software include the physical and digital tools necessary for project execution. Consistency involves maintaining regular effort and performance, while delegation allows distributing tasks to leverage the strengths of others, ensuring that the workload is manageable.

Ultimately, the workforce comprises the human resources necessary to bring the project to fruition. The support and collaboration of a dedicated team are not just beneficial, but it's crucial. It can significantly enhance the chances of success and make the journey more enjoyable. (wheelawaysales.com) Combining these mandatory tools provides a comprehensive framework that empowers individuals to accomplish their dreams, goals, and purposes. By following this roadmap, one can navigate the complexities of any project and achieve outstanding results.

References

Wheel Away Sales.com, Succeeding With The Right Advice.
https://wheelawaysales.com/succeed-with-this-advice/

About The Author

84

About The Author

Brenda Diann Johnson was born in Dallas, Texas on September 14, 1970 to Robert Johnson and Thelma Byrd. She is the oldest of five children. She has a brother, sister, and two half brothers.

Brenda received her education from the Dallas and Wharton, Texas school systems. She graduated from Government, Law, and Law Enforcement Magnet High School in Dallas. She also received her Bachelor of Arts degree in Communications (Broadcast News) from UTA in Arlington, Texas and her Masters of Education Degree from Strayer University. She has her Texas license in Life, Health, Accident & HMO insurance, her Texas Adjusters License in All Lines, and she is a Texas Notary Public.

Today, Brenda is the CEO/Founder of The Young Scholar's Book Club and ASWIFTT ENTERPRISES, LLC. She is also an experienced educator who has taught and tutored Pre-K through College. Brenda is the Dean of Education, Curriculum & Instruction for Best Practices Training Institute (B.P.T.I). She has also authored books and articles.

From 2001 to 2002, Brenda served as the chairperson for an entrepreneur group called STEP (Sowing Toward Everlasting Prosperity) and as a Center Leader for the Plan Fund.

She also served as the Co-Founder of ASWIFTT Writer's Guild from 2010 to 2019.

In the community, she has served as a volunteer to organizations that help AIDS, HIV, and Syphilis patients.

Brenda currently lives in Texas with her family.

Books and Services
ASWIFTT ENTERPRISES, LLC

Business advertising for Print & Media
BOOK PUBLISHING
RADIO
T.V.
Newspaper

We have affordable advertising packages in our media categories. Some Ads are as low as $35.00. Email to ask about our Business Ads and Commercials.

You can visit us online or e-mail us:
www.aswifttbooks.com
aswifttbookpublishing@yahoo.com

ASWIFTT BOOKS

(Ambassadors Sent With Information For This Time)

ASWIFTT ENTERPRISES, LLC creates businesses that write and publish in all three (3) media genres such as radio, tv, and newspaper that focus on delivering timely, newsworthy and accurate news stories. The media genres also report on local, regional, national and international topics.

The Young Scholar's Workbook:
Book I Vol. I (www.tysbookclub.com)

The Young Scholar's Workbook: Book I Vol. I

By Brenda Diann Johnson

This is a fundraiser publication for The Young Scholar's Book Club. 50% of the proceeds go to help keep mentoring and tutoring services free to students. $19.95 plus s/h

How Did I Get Into This Mess?
You Compromised, Saith the Lord
2nd Edition

How Did I Get Into This Mess? You Compromised, Saith the Lord 2nd Edition by Brenda Diann Johnson

$12.95 plus s/h

Articles for Personal Growth and Development: Volume I

Articles for Personal Growth and Development: Vol. I by

Brenda Diann Johnson

$9.95 plus s/h

My Baby Sister

My Baby Sister by

Brenda Diann Johnson

$15.95 plus s/h

Available in English and Spanish

Advertise in
ASWIFTT BOOKS

Your business will have a permanent advertising spot in an ASWIFTT Book. The book that carries your Business Ad will continue to advertise your business every time the book is printed and purchased by a customer. For more information on ASWIFTT ENTERPRISES book advertising email us at: aswifttbookpublishing@yahoo.com

$35.00 Business Ad
Includes:
Business Name
Address

$100.00 Business Ad
Includes:
Logo
Business Name
Address
Phone Number
Website
Short Bio

$65.00 Business Ad
Includes:
Logo
Business Name
Address
Phone Number
Website

ASWIFTT ENTERPRISES, LLC ORDER FORM

Name_____

Address_____

City_____

State_____

Zip_____
Item _____Amount_____
Item _____Amount_____
Item _____Amount_____

Add $8.50 for Shipping and Handling on books
Total:_____

Make Checks, Money Orders, Cashier's Checks out to:

ASWIFTT ENTERPRISES, LLC

P.O. Box 380669

Duncanville, Texas 75138

Credit Card Orders:
Circle One: Master Card   Visa   American Express Discover
Credit Card Number_____
Exp. Date_____
Three Digit Security Number on back of Card_____

Name & Address Associated with Credit Card:

Authorization Signature_____Date_____

Your order will be processed or shipped 2 to 4 weeks from the date order is received. Direct concerns on orders email: aswifttbookpublishing@yahoo.com
You can also order online at: www.aswifttbooks.com

Thank you for your business! Make copies of this form.

www.ingramcontent.com/pod-product-compliance
Lightning Source LLC
Chambersburg PA
CBHW060848050426
42453CB00008B/900